★ THE MONKEY KING'S SACRIFICE

FRIENDS! WE HAVE BEEN LIVING HAPPILY ON THIS MANGO TREE FOR YEARS.

BUT I ANTICIPATE TROUBLE, SOON.

WHY MASTER?

MEN HAVE COME TO LIVE NEAR OUR FOREST. THEY HAVE NEVER TASTED THE MANGO FRUIT.

★ BASED ON MAHA KAPI JATAKA

ONCE THEY DO, IT WILL BE DANGEROUS FOR US.

OH DEAR! WHAT SHALL WE DO?

MAKE SURE THAT NOT A SINGLE FRUIT FALLS INTO THE RIVER.

PLUCK EACH AND EVERY BUD FROM THE BRANCHES THAT SPREAD OUT OVER THE RIVER.

BUT IN SPITE OF ALL THIS CARE, A JUICY RIPE MANGO FELL INTO THE RIVER...

SPLAT

... AND GOT CAUGHT IN A FISHERMAN'S NET.

WHEN HE GOT HOME AND BEGAN SORTING OUT THE FISH—

LOOK! SEE WHAT I HAVE FOUND AMONG THE FISH. A STRANGE FRUIT. IT LOOKS DELICIOUS!

I HAVE NEVER SEEN A FRUIT LIKE THAT BEFORE.

I THINK WE OUGHT TO TAKE IT TO THE KING.

YES. I THINK I'D BETTER.

SO, ALONG WITH A FRIEND, HE SET OFF FOR THE KING'S PALACE.

THE KING WILL BE OVERJOYED WHEN HE SEES IT.

THEY REACHED THE PALACE LATE THAT NIGHT.

HALT

WE'D LIKE TO SHOW THIS FRUIT TO THE KING.

THEY WERE LET IN.

OH MASTER, THIS FRUIT WAS AMONG THE FISH I CAUGHT.

HM-M!

SEND FOR THE FORESTER. HE WILL TELL US WHAT FRUIT IT IS.

THAT'S THE RARE MANGO, SIR.

IS IT POISONOUS?

NOT AT ALL, SIR. IN FACT IT IS VERY TASTY.

SO THE KING SUNK HIS TEETH INTO IT.

HM-M-M! DELICIOUS.

IT SMELLS GOOD, TOO!

NEXT MORNING —

TELL ME FORESTER, WHERE DOES THIS MANGO FRUIT GROW.

THERE IS A MANGO GROVE, JUST A LITTLE UPSTREAM, SIR.

MINISTER, MAKE THE NECESSARY ARRANGEMENTS. WE ARE LEAVING FOR THAT GROVE.

YES, SIR.

SOON THEY WERE OFF.

I HOPE YOU HAVE BROUGHT SOME ARCHERS ALONG.

I HAVE, SIR.

WHEN THEY REACHED THE SPOT —

TELL EVERYONE TO EAT AS MUCH AS THEY CAN.

MINISTER, WE WILL STAY HERE FOR A DAY OR TWO.

I WILL MAKE THE ARRANGEMENTS, SIR.

AS NIGHT FELL, THE MONKEYS BEGAN MOVING ABOUT.

MINISTER, WHAT WAS THAT?

JUST MONKEYS SIR, SCAMPERING AMONG THE BRANCHES.

WHEN IT'S MORNING, TELL THE ARCHERS TO SHOOT EVERY SINGLE MONKEY.

I SHALL, SIR.

THE NEXT MORNING—

TODAY ALONG WITH THE MANGOES WE SHALL EAT MONKEY'S FLESH.

OH MASTER, WE'RE TRAPPED.

WHAT ARE WE TO DO NOW ?

EYOW

DON'T PANIC. I'LL FIND A WAY OUT.

THEY MANAGED TO GET TO A TREE NEAR THE RIVER.

NOW ALL OF YOU DO AS I TELL YOU.

HE GOT HOLD OF A THICK LONG CREEPER. HE TIED ONE END OF IT TO A BRANCH AND THE OTHER TO HIS WAIST.

NOW I WILL SWING OVER THE RIVER TO THAT FIG TREE ON THE OPPOSITE BANK. ONE BY ONE YOU CAN COME ACROSS TO THE OTHER SIDE.

OH NO! THE VINE IS TOO SHORT.

I WILL TRY TO GET HOLD OF THIS BRANCH AND BRIDGE THE GAP.

LOOK AT THAT MONKEY KING. HOW HE MUST LOVE HIS SUBJECTS.

THE MONKEYS BEGAN CROSSING.

WHAT ARE YOU WAITING FOR? CROSS OVER MY BACK.

BUT, MASTER, HOW CAN I...

THIS IS NO TIME TO THINK ABOUT SUCH THINGS. CROSS QUICKLY.

YOU ARE VERY KIND, MASTER.

ALL THE MONKEYS CROSSED OVER IN THIS MANNER. THE LAST ONE WAS A WICKED MONKEY WHO HAD NEVER LIKED HIS KING.

HERE IS MY CHANCE TO TAKE REVENGE

I SHALL JUMP ACROSS AND PUSH HIM DOWN.

COME ON. PLEASE HURRY.

WHEN THEY GOT TO THE OTHER SIDE —

YOU SAVED THEM AT THE COST OF YOUR OWN LIFE!

I DON'T MIND. I HAVE DONE MY DUTY.

LET ME TAKE YOU BACK AND LOOK AFTER YOU.

NO. PLEASE LEAVE ME HERE. I AM ABOUT TO DIE.

NOBLE SOUL! HOW PAINFUL IT MUST ALL BE.

I DON'T MIND THE PAIN. I AM HAPPY THAT MY SUBJECTS ARE SAFE.

★THE STUPID CROCODILE AND THE MONKEY

IN A DENSE JUNGLE, NEAR A RIVER, THERE LIVED A CLEVER LITTLE MONKEY.

HM! I'M HUNGRY.

IN THE MIDDLE OF THE RIVER WAS A SMALL ISLAND, WHERE PLENTY OF DELICIOUS FRUITS GREW. WHENEVER THE MONKEY FELT HUNGRY, HE WENT STRAIGHT TO THE ISLAND.

★ BASED ON VANARINDA JATAKA

HE WOULD JUMP FROM THE BANK, ONTO A ROCK IN THE RIVER AND THEN TO THE SMALL ISLAND.

BREAKFAST. HERE I COME!

HMM! NOTHING LIKE FRUIT FOR A HEALTHY BREAKFAST.

HUH...

?

PUCH

ROTTEN FRUIT!

I WONDER WHERE IT CAME FROM.

PUCH

OH WELL! ONE MUST TAKE THE GOOD WITH THE BAD!

NOT FAR AWAY THERE LIVED A CROCODILE AND HIS WIFE.

YOU KNOW DEAR, I'VE GOT IT! I KNOW HOW WE CAN CATCH THAT LITTLE MONKEY FOR OUR DINNER.

OH PLEASE! NOT AGAIN. WE'VE TRIED IT TOO MANY TIMES BEFORE. LET US BE HAPPY WITH THE FISH I CATCH.

THIS TIME MY PLAN WON'T FAIL. I PROMISE.

SO THEY CAUTIOUSLY APPROACHED THE SPOT WHERE THE MONKEY LIVED.

YOU SEE THAT ROCK THERE? THE MONKEY USES IT TO REACH THE ISLAND.

SHH! QUIET. HE MIGHT HEAR YOU.

WHEN HE'S ON THE ISLAND, BUSY EATING HIS BREAKFAST, YOU LIE ON THAT ROCK. WHEN HE HAS TO RETURN, HE WILL THINK YOU'RE THE ROCK. AS SOON AS HE JUMPS ON YOU, KILL HIM.

HMM! THE PLAN SOUNDS GOOD.

THE NEXT DAY AS USUAL THE MONKEY SET OUT FOR THE ISLAND.

I'M HUNGRY!

SO AM I! HEE! HEE!

WHEN HE HAD EATEN TO HIS STOMACH'S CONTENT—

HEY! THAT'S STRANGE! THAT ROCK LOOKS BIGGER TODAY.

THE RIVER HAS NOT GONE DRY FOR IT TO LOOK BIGGER.

I'M SURE IT IS THAT STUPID CROCODILE, UP TO HIS TRICKS AGAIN. I WON'T JUMP TILL I'M SURE.

LET ME SEE IF THIS IDEA WORKS.

HELLO ROCK! HOW ARE YOU TODAY, MY FRIEND?

THE MONKEY CALLED OVER AND OVER AGAIN.

WHY AREN'T YOU SPEAKING TO ME TODAY ROCK? HAVE I ANNOYED YOU?

IT LOOKS AS IF THIS ROCK USED TO TALK TO HIM. I'D BETTER REPLY.

?

AS THE MONKEY HAD EXPECTED, THE MOMENT THE CROCODILE OPENED HIS MOUTH WIDE, HIS EYES CLOSED.

NOW'S MY CHANCE. I'LL JUMP ON HIM AND ONTO THE BANK. I'LL HAVE TO BE QUICK.

TAKE THAT!

THUD

WHAT WAS THAT?

WHAT ARE YOU DOING OVER THERE? YOU PROMISED YOU WOULD JUMP INTO MY MOUTH.

DID YOU REALLY BELIEVE I'D DO A STUPID THING LIKE THAT?

GRR! WAIT TILL I GET MY TEETH INTO YOU.

YOU NEVER WILL, CROCODILE. YOU MAY BE BIG AND STRONG BUT YOU ARE STUPID.

★THE DEMON OUTWITTED

LONG AGO A BAND OF MONKEYS CAME AND SETTLED ON THE OUTSKIRTS OF A FOREST.

THE LEADER WHO KNEW THE PLACE WELL, CALLED A MEETING.

ATTENTION, ALL OF YOU! I HAVE SOMETHING IMPORTANT TO SAY.

YOU WILL HAVE TO BE CAREFUL ABOUT TWO THINGS IN THIS FOREST.

THERE ARE CERTAIN POISONOUS TREES WITH VERY TEMPTING FRUIT AND ONE OF THE LAKES IS HAUNTED BY A DEMON.

17　　　★ BASED ON NALAPANA JATAKA

YOU MUST NOT DRINK WATER OR EAT ANY FRUIT WITHOUT ASKING ME.

ONE DAY WHILE SEARCHING FOR FIREWOOD, THE MONKEYS WANDERED DEEP INTO THE FOREST.

MOTHER, I'M THIRSTY.

AH! THERE IS A LAKE CLOSE BY.

WAIT! DON'T GO NEAR THE WATER.

DON'T YOU REMEMBER OUR LEADER'S WARNING?

OH DEAR! I'D COMPLETELY FORGOTTEN. THANK YOU FOR REMINDING ME.

ALL RIGHT! LET US WAIT TILL OUR LEADER COMES.

A LITTLE LATER —

AH! HERE HE IS.

WHAT'S THE MATTER? YOU SEEM TO HAVE A PROBLEM.

MASTER, WE ARE VERY THIRSTY.

WE ARE WAITING FOR YOU TO LET US KNOW IF THIS LAKE IS SAFE.

THAT WAS VERY WISE OF YOU. NOW LET ME EXAMINE THE LAKE.

HMM! ALL THE FOOTSTEPS LEAD **INTO** THE LAKE.

BUT NOT A SINGLE ONE LEADS OUT OF IT.

COLLECT ALL THE BAMBOO REEDS YOU CAN.

HM..M...M... THIS ONE'S FINE. ABSOLUTELY HOLLOW.

WHAT ABOUT THIS ONE?

EXCELLENT. IT FITS INTO THE OTHER PERFECTLY.

THUS BY JOINING A NUMBER OF THE REEDS TOGETHER THE LEADER MADE ONE LONG HOLLOW REED.

NOW I'LL SLIDE THAT END INTO THE WATER.

NOW WHAT?

I'LL SUCK THE WATER FROM THIS END.

AND WITH ALL HIS MIGHT HE SUCKED AT THE REED TILL...

SKURRRRR

... THE WATER GUSHED OUT IN A THICK STREAM.

SPLAT

WATER! DELICIOUS WATER! AND ALL FOR US.

FULL OF RAGE, THE OUTWITTED DEMON STOMPED BACK INTO THE LAKE.

GRRRR!

HA HA HA HO HO HEE HO HA HA

AND THE MONKEYS THEIR THIRST WELL QUENCHED, RETURNED HOME.

23

* **BASED ON SUMSUMARA JATAKA**

I'D BETTER THINK FAST IF I LOVE MY LIFE.

HA! HA! HA! HO! HO! HEE! HEEE! THE JOKE'S ON YOU, CROCODILE.

STOP THAT. WHAT'S SO FUNNY ABOUT DYING?

YOU MAY KILL ME. BUT YOU WILL NEVER GET MY HEART.

WHAT DO YOU MEAN?

WE MONKEYS HIDE OUR HEARTS IN SAFE PLACES BEFORE WE VENTURE OUT.

REALLY? HOW WAS I TO KNOW?

* THE MONKEYS AND THE GARDENER

THE KING OF VARANASI HAD A BEAUTIFUL GARDEN, WHICH WAS LOOKED AFTER BY A LOYAL GARDENER.

ONE NIGHT —

HELLO FRIEND. THE FESTIVAL IN TOWN BEGINS TOMORROW.

I KNOW!

THERE'S GOING TO BE PLENTY OF FUN.

HOW I WISH I COULD COME!

WHAT! AREN'T YOU COMING?

IF I DO, WHO WILL WATER THE GARDEN?

28

★ BASED ON ARMADUSAKA JATAKA

MEANWHILE IN TOWN —

I WONDER HOW MY MONKEY FRIENDS ARE GETTING ALONG WITH THEIR TASK?

TWO DAYS LATER THE GARDENER RETURNED HOME.

?!

WHAT HAVE YOU DONE?

WE WATERED EACH PLANT ACCORDING TO THE NEEDS OF ITS ROOTS

THAT'S RIGHT. WE DID.

WHATEVER, SHALL I DO NOW? WHAT SHALL I TELL THE KING?

THAT'S WHAT COMES OF DEPENDING ON A FOOL. HE MAY MEAN WELL BUT WILL END UP DOING MORE HARM THAN ANYTHING ELSE.